Cambridge Discovery Readers

Level 2

Series editor: Nicholas Tims

New Zealand

Margaret Johnson

T0349515

CAMBRIDGE
UNIVERSITY PRESS

CAMBRIDGE UNIVERSITY PRESS
Cambridge, New York, Melbourne, Madrid, Cape Town,
Singapore, São Paulo, Delhi, Tokyo, Mexico City

Cambridge University Press
79 Anson Road, #06-04/06, Singapore 079906

www.cambridge.org
Information on this title: www.cambridge.org/9780521149020

This American English edition is based on *New Zealand*, ISBN 978-8-483-23488-4
first published by Cambridge University Press in 2009.

First published 2009
American English edition 2010
Reprinted 2011

Printed in Singapore by Tien Wah Press

ISBN 978-0-521-14902-0 Paperback American English edition

No character in this work is based on any person living or dead.
Any resemblance to an actual person or situation is purely accidental.

Illustrations by Christophe Berthoud (Beehive Illustration) and El Ojo del Huracán

Audio recording by hyphen

The publishers are grateful to the following for permission to reproduce
photographic material on the cover:

Hulton Archive/Getty Images; istockphoto.com/©David Mathies

Contents

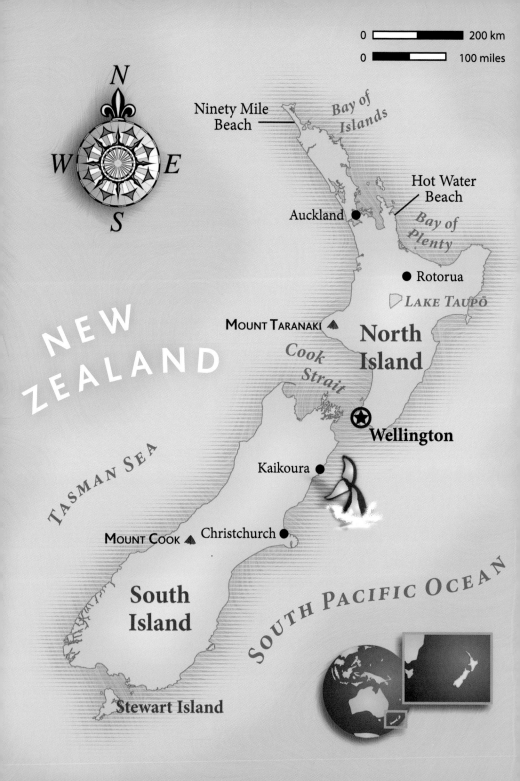

Introduction

New Zealand is in the South Pacific Ocean, a long way from anywhere. Australia is the closest country and that's two thousand kilometers away. New Zealand is isolated and this makes it special. This isolation changes everything – New Zealand's history, the weather, the way its people are, and the trees, flowers, and animals that you can see.

New Zealand is made up of two large islands – the North Island and the South Island, and a much smaller island, Stewart Island. It is about the same size as the United Kingdom, but it has only four million people. The United Kingdom has sixty-one million people. There are almost a million young people under fifteen in New Zealand.

The main language of New Zealand is English. New Zealand was once part of the British Empire and still has the British flag as part of its own flag.

The weather in New Zealand is never usually really hot or really cold, but it is hotter on the North Island where most people live (about three million people live on this island). It often rains and the weather can change quickly. Sometimes you can get many different kinds of weather in one day, especially on the South Island.

New Zealand has a lot of water, clean air, and good earth and there are many farms. It is famous for its butter, cheese, and meat, which it sells to Australia, the U.S.A., Japan, and the rest of Asia.

There are forty million sheep in the country – that's ten for every person!

For a long time, no people lived in New Zealand. The first people to make New Zealand their home were the Māori. They arrived from Polynesia in boats made of wood, called *waka*. We don't know when they arrived, but some people think it was between 950–1130 AD. The Māori called New Zealand *Aotearoa*, or "Land of the Long White Cloud." Around the year 1700, Europeans first came to New Zealand.

Today thousands of people go to New Zealand on vacation. They go to see the beautiful countryside and to enjoy sports. While they are there, tourists can also learn about the Māori and hear many Māori stories about New Zealand. The biggest business in New Zealand is now tourism.

How mountains and volcanoes began

Maui was a boy who could do magic[1]. One day he wanted to go fishing with his older brothers. He hid in the bottom of his brothers' waka. Once out at sea, Maui's brothers found him. They wanted to take him back to the village because he was too young, but Maui quickly used his magic. He made his village look very far away – too far to go home. His brothers had to let him stay.

When Maui and his brothers started fishing, Maui decided to use his magic again. Soon he felt something very strong pulling on his fishing line.

"Help me!" Maui called to his brothers and they all came to help.

Everyone pulled very hard until they pulled up the North Island of New Zealand.

Maui didn't want the gods to be angry with them for doing this and he moved away from his brothers to talk to the gods quietly. But while he was gone, his brothers began to argue over the island.

"It's mine!" one shouted.

"No, it's mine!" the other said.

They became so angry they began to hit the island. Hit, hit, hit – over and over again. As they hit it, they made the mountains and volcanoes[2] of the North Island.

The Māori believe that the North Island looks like a fish, the South Island looks like Maui's waka, and Stewart Island looks like the waka's anchor[3].

ACTIVITIES

1 Match these facts from the Introduction with the numbers.

1 kilometers between New Zealand and Australia ☐ *b*
2 people in New Zealand ☐
3 people in the United Kingdom ☐
4 people under fifteen in New Zealand ☐
5 people who live on the North Island ☐
6 sheep in New Zealand ☐

a almost 1,000,000
~~b~~ 2,000
c 3,000,000
d 4,000,000
e 40,000,000
f 61,000,000

2 Use information from the Introduction to answer the questions.

1 What is the main language in New Zealand?
   English.
2 What is the climate like there?
   ....
3 What food is New Zealand famous for?
   ....
4 What do the Māori people call New Zealand?
   ....
5 When did people from Europe first come to New Zealand?
   ....
6 What is the biggest business in New Zealand today?
   ....

Chapter 1

The Māori

The early Māori were gardeners and farmers. They brought plants and animals with them from Polynesia in their waka. Some of the plants did not like New Zealand's colder weather.

The Māori began to kill the birds for food. One of these was the moa bird, which was almost three meters high. There are no moa birds alive today – people say the Māori killed them all. They liked to cook food in ovens under the earth called *hāngi*. It takes a long time to cook meat and vegetables in a hāngi.

The Māori believed in gods, and told stories about these gods' lives. Stories have always been very important for the Māori people. Their stories explain the beginning of the world. The Māori always sang or spoke these stories. Over the years, people told these same stories to their children and their children told them to their children. We call this an oral culture[4].

FACT

When Europeans arrived in New Zealand, fighting and illness killed a lot of Māori until there were only 42,113 of them in the country. Today there are over 600,000.

Māori art

The Māori are famous for their woodcarving. When they arrived in New Zealand, they found large trees everywhere. They used stone or bone tools to carve[5] the wood from these trees. The Māori carved pictures on most things they used. Like Māori songs, the carvings tell Māori stories. The Māori built beautiful meeting houses called *wharenuis* and these are full of carvings. The most famous of these is in the Te Papa Tongarewa National Museum in Wellington.

The Māori are also famous for the art they put on their faces. They often painted their faces with pictures or tattoos, called *moko*. Women had tattoos on their lips, chin, and sometimes arms. Men had tattoos all over their faces. Some Māori people have these tattoos today. When you get a tattoo, it hurts a lot. A woman's lip and chin tattoo can take six hours.

The Māori wore grass skirts called *piupiu*. The women also wore colorful tops called *pari*. They were often red, black, and white. Māori women made these clothes, using weaving[6].

On Rotorua, on the North Island, you can visit Te Puia, which is the New Zealand Māori Arts and Crafts Institute. Here you can see how the Māori lived. You can also watch young Māori people at the carving school. Twelve students study at the carving school for three years to learn how to carve. Other young students learn how to weave.

How Mataora learned to do tattoos

Mataora, a young Māori man, fell in love with Niwareka. Niwareka lived in the Underworld, a place under the earth, but she agreed to come up above the earth to live with Mataora. But Mataora wasn't always very nice to Niwareka and she became unhappy. She decided to go back under the earth to be with her father.

Mataora felt bad without Niwareka. He loved her and wanted her to come back. So he decided to go to the Underworld to speak to her. Mataora painted his face to look good, but as he went under the earth, the paint came off. When he arrived in the Underworld and found Niwareka, Mataora knew he didn't look good at all, but he spoke to her anyway. He told her he was very sorry and that he loved her. Niwareka listened to him. She loved him too, so she agreed to return with him.

Before they left, Niwareka's father tattooed Mataora's face. Then he showed him how to do tattoos for other people. When he was home, all Mataora's friends liked his tattoos and wanted to have them, too.

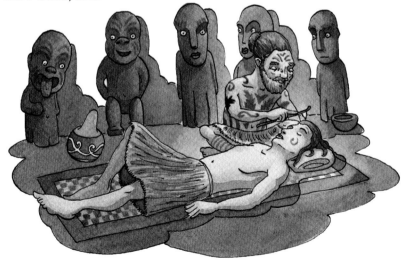

ACTIVITIES

1 <u>Underline</u> the correct answer to complete the definitions of these Māori words.

1 The moa is a ... .

a boat   b <u>bird</u>   c tree

2 A hāngi is a place for ... .

a meeting   b carving   c cooking

3 A wharenui is a ... .

a song   b building   c woodcarving

4 A moko is a ... .

a tattoo   b story   c skirt

5 A piupiu is a ... .

a skirt   b tool   c carving

6 A pari is a ... for women.

a tattoo   b tool   c top

2 Are the sentences true (*T*) or false (*F*)?

1 The Māori killed moa birds to give to the gods. ☐F☐

2 For the Māori, stories about their gods' lives explain how the world began. ☐

3 The Māori only tell their stories through singing. ☐

4 The Māori wrote their stories. ☐

5 The Māori carved pictures on most things they used. ☐

6 Māori people do not have tattoos today. ☐

Chapter 2

Birds, animals, trees, and flowers

The kiwi

The most famous bird in New Zealand is the kiwi. Most kiwi birds are brown and about the same size as a chicken. The kiwi is famous because it cannot fly. People from New Zealand are often called Kiwis because of their famous bird.

FACT

One of the most famous Kiwis was Sir Edmund Hillary (1919–2008). Hillary and Sherpa Tenzing Norgay were the first people to climb Mount Everest, the world's highest mountain, in 1953.

Kiwi birds cannot fly because hundreds of years ago, there were no animals in New Zealand except bats[7] and ocean animals like dolphins. The kiwi did not need to fly to get away from anything. It was safe.

Kiwi birds cannot see very well. They find food by smelling it. They are the only birds in the world with nostrils at the end of their long bill. In some ways, they are more like a land animal than a bird. If anyone comes near, they run away. Then they stand and smell the air to see if it is safe.

Kiwi birds are difficult to see, because they are the color of the earth. They live in thick trees in quiet areas and they come out at night, not in the day. Most New Zealanders have only seen them in a zoo.

Now the kiwi is an endangered[8] bird. This is because of the animals the first people to come to New Zealand brought with them. Some of these animals got into the countryside and began to kill and eat the kiwi birds.

People also cut down many of the trees the kiwi likes to live in. Today there are now only seventy thousand birds left in the country.

There are conservation groups working to help the kiwi. Young people can help too, and the Ministry of Youth organizes conservation training and work experience for people aged 16–25.

How the kiwi lost its wings

One day, Tāne Mahuta, the god of trees and birds, looked up at the trees and saw that something was eating them. The trees looked sick. He looked more closely and saw that the trees had insects all over them. The insects were eating the trees.

Tāne Mahuta had a meeting with all the birds.

"Insects are eating the trees," he told them. "I need one of you to come down from the treetops and live on the floor under the trees. You have to eat the insects to save the trees. Who will come?"

All was quiet. None of the birds spoke.

Tāne Mahuta asked the birds again.

"Will you come down from the trees?"

Tui answered first. He said it was too dark on the ground and he was afraid of the dark.

Then Pūkeko said the ground was too wet and he didn't want to get his feet wet.

Lastly, Pipiwharauroa said he was too busy making a nest – a home for his family.

Tāne Mahuta felt very sad. He didn't want the trees to die. He turned to the kiwi bird.

"Kiwi," he asked. "Will you come down from the trees?"

Kiwi looked up at the trees and saw the sun. He looked around and saw his family. He looked down at the cold, wet earth. Then he turned to Tāne Mahuta and said sadly, "I will."

Tāne Mahuta was very happy when he heard this, but he also felt sad for Kiwi. He wanted Kiwi to know what he was agreeing to.

"Kiwi," he said, "if you do this, your legs will become thick and strong. You will lose your beautiful colors and you will never return to the top of the trees. You will never see the light of day again. Kiwi, will you come down from the trees?"

Kiwi looked at the sun on the trees again and said goodbye. Then he looked sadly at Tāne Mahuta. "I will," he said.

Tāne Mahuta smiled at Kiwi. Then he looked at the other birds. "Tui," he said, "because you didn't agree to come down from the trees, you will wear two white feathers to show you were afraid. Pūkeko, because you did not want to get your feet wet, you will always live in the swamp[9]. Pipiwharauroa, because you were too busy building your nest, you will never build another nest again. You will put your eggs in other birds' nests."

Then Tāne Mahuta smiled at Kiwi again.

"Kiwi," he said, "because you said yes, you will become the most well-known and best-loved bird of all."

The kakapo parrot

Another New Zealand bird that cannot fly is the kakapo parrot. The kakapo parrot is green and gray and is the world's heaviest parrot. It makes a very loud sound and it can live up to ninety years. Kakapos lived on Stewart Island without anyone knowing about them until 1845.

There are even fewer kakapos left than kiwis – not more than a hundred in the country! The people working to save these birds have given them all names. Between 1982 and 1997, people took the parrots to live on small islands where there were no animals to eat them.

Whales

There are lots of whales in the water around New Zealand. This is because the oceans and seas are full of the food that whales like. Whales are the biggest animals in the world – they can grow to be thirty-five meters long.

In the past, people often killed whales in New Zealand. People ate whale meat and also used the oil from the whales' bodies. Today both people in New Zealand and tourists like watching the whales, not killing them. Kaikoura, in the east of the South Island, is a good place to see them. When the whales come up to get some air, they send water right up into the sky. People get very excited when they see it.

The kauri tree

Since New Zealand is a long way from anywhere, it has many trees and flowers that you don't find in other places in the world. New Zealand's best-known tree is the kauri, which can live for as long as two thousand years. It can grow up to fifty meters tall. The Māori used it to make their waka. Europeans also used the kauri tree to make their houses. There are still some of these houses in the older parts of Wellington, the capital of New Zealand. Northland, at the top of the North Island, is a good place to see the kauri and it is here that a tree called Tāne Mahuta (the same name as the god of trees) grows. Tāne Mahuta is New Zealand's tallest tree. It is 51.2 meters tall.

ACTIVITIES

1 Match the words in the box to the sentences.

| kiwis (x4) kakapos (x4) whales (x2) |

1 There are seventy thousand _kiwis_ left in New Zealand.
2 There are under a hundred .... left.
3 .... can live for ninety years.
4 .... find food by smelling it.
5 .... are green and gray in color.
6 Kaikoura is a good place to see ....
7 People ate .... in the past.
8 People from New Zealand have the same name: ....
9 .... are the heaviest of their kind in the world.
10 .... are the same size as a chicken.

2 Match the stories in the box, from the Introduction and Chapters 1 and 2, with the sentences.

| Maui story (x2)   Mataora story   Tāne Mahuta story |

1 There is a family fight in this story. ....
2 This story tells how New Zealand's birds became the way they are. ....
3 Three brothers help to make New Zealand in this story.
   .... _Maui story_ ....
4 Someone learns to do something in this story.
   ....

Chapter 3

Mountains and the big outdoors

Tramps

New Zealand is famous for its mountains and its countryside. There are mountains in sixty percent of the South Island and twenty percent of the North Island. Over three-quarters of New Zealand's people live in cities, but they are never very far from the countryside. Many Kiwis enjoy going on walks or, as they say, "tramps." People who come on vacation to New Zealand often like to go on tramps, too. It is a good way to learn about the country and an excellent way to see how beautiful it is.

There are many different tramps to go on in New Zealand. Some are along beaches and some are through trees. Some are next to rivers and some are in the mountains of the South Island or the volcanoes of the North Island. If you go on tramps near volcanoes, there are often hot springs – places where there are pools with hot water from volcanoes.

One tramp near hot springs is from the Waikato River to the Huka Falls. The water here can be up to 22°C. At Wai-O-Tapu, or Lady Knox Geyser, on the North Island, water goes ten meters into the air every day at 10:15 a.m. Places where there are volcanoes often smell bad – a little like old eggs!

How Tongariro won Pihanga

Many years ago, five mountains lived together in the center of the North Island. Four of them were male – Tongariro, Taranaki, Tauhara, and Pūtauaki. The other, Pihanga, was female.

Pihanga was a round mountain with soft, green clothes. All the male mountains loved her. One day they had a big fight about her. It was a hard fight, but finally Tongariro won. Right away, he put his soft cloud arms around Pihanga. Then he told the other male mountains to leave.

Mountains can only move at night, so they all had to move quickly while the sun was down. Tauhara and Pūtauaki decided to travel to the ocean. But Tauhara was so sad to be leaving Pihanga, he kept stopping to look back at her. By the time the sun came up, he was only by Lake Taupō. Pūtauaki was very close to the ocean.

Taranaki was so angry with Tongariro that he moved away very quickly. When the sun came up, he was at the far west of the island. Today he still looks back and shouts at Tongariro, who won the fight for Pihanga.

Most tramps take between three and five days. People who go on tramps often carry their things in a bag on their back – in a backpack. Trampers usually sleep in tents or trampers' huts[10]. If you stay in a trampers' hut, you are often with other young people. It can be a lot of fun to meet young people from New Zealand and other countries, and to talk about the tramps you are doing.

The Te Araroa Trust is making a new path[11] right now. This will cross all of New Zealand, from Cape Reinga at the top of the North Island to Bluff on the South Island. It will be three thousand kilometers long. Its name will be Long Pathway, or Te Araroa.

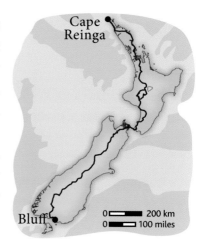

FACT

New Zealand's mountains are around five million years old. This makes them very young mountains. The oldest mountains in the world are over three billion years old!

Mount Cook, on the South Island, is New Zealand's highest mountain at 3,754 meters. New Zealand's mountains are not very high, but they can be difficult to climb. Sir Edmund Hillary learned how to climb by climbing New Zealand's mountains.

You can also climb New Zealand's volcanoes – for example, Mount Taranaki on the North Island, which is 2,518 meters high. Most climbers in New Zealand climb mountains in the warmer months. Since New Zealand is in the Southern Hemisphere, the summer months are December, January, and February.

On the west of the South Island there are glaciers to walk on or climb. These are Fox Glacier and Franz Josef Glacier. They are like cold mountains of ice.

Skiing

Another way to enjoy the mountains is to go skiing. Skiing is important to Kiwis and there are lots of places to go skiing – on both the North and the South Islands.

Some people think Turoa and Whakapapa are the best places to go skiing. Both are active[12] volcanoes on the North Island on Mount Ruapehu. There are not many places in the world where you can ski on an active volcano!

Beach life

If you like to be outdoors but do not like to be so energetic, New Zealand has a very large coastline. For Kiwis, going to the beach is a part of daily life. They love swimming in the ocean and cooking food outside on a barbecue.

Ninety Mile Beach is the longest beach in New Zealand. Ninety miles is about 145 kilometers. Kiwis do not know how the beach got its name because the beach is only sixty miles (ninety-seven kilometers) long!

Hot Water Beach, on the east coast of the North Island, is a very unusual place. Hot water up to 64°C comes up out of the sand. You can make a hole and sit in the hot water while the cold ocean comes in over your legs!

ACTIVITIES

1 Complete the sentences with the numbers in the box.

| 2,518 | 3,000 | 3,754 |
| 5,000,000 | ~~60~~ | 64 | 97 |

1 About ....60.... percent of the South Island is made up of mountains.
2 The temperature of the water at Hot Water Beach can get to .... degrees Celsius.
3 The new path from Cape Reinga to Bluff will be .... kilometers long.
4 New Zealand's mountains are about .... years old.
5 Mount Cook is .... meters high.
6 Mount Taranaki is .... meters high.
7 The longest beach is .... kilometers long.

2 Match the two parts of the sentences about the Māori story on pages 24–5.
1 Five mountains lived together ☑ d
2 Four of the mountains were male ☐
3 All the male mountains ☐
4 There was a fight about Pihanga ☐

a and one of them was female.
b and the mountain Tongariro won.
c loved Pihanga, the female.
d in the center of the North Island.

Chapter 4

Sports

Rugby

Kiwis love sports. The most important sport in New Zealand is rugby.

Lots of young people play or watch rugby in the winter. A man named Charles Monro brought rugby to New Zealand from Great Britain in the late 1860s. There are fifteen players on a rugby team. A rugby ball is not round, like a soccer ball – it is an oval shape, a little like an egg.

New Zealand's national rugby team is the famous All Blacks. They got their name when they started to wear black shorts and rugby shirts. The All Blacks have won against all the world's best rugby teams. When the All Blacks are playing, the streets in New Zealand are almost empty. Everyone is inside, watching the game on television.

The tallest All Black was 2.05 meters.
The shortest All Black was 1.6 meters.
The heaviest All Black was 130 kilos.
The lightest All Black was 59 kilos.

As well as being famous for winning, the All Blacks are famous for their special dance – called a *haka*. The haka is a Māori dance with loud shouting. The All Blacks dance a haka called Ka Mate before a rugby game begins, while the other team stands and watches. The haka is sung in the Māori language. It is a very strong, loud dance and maybe the All Blacks hope the other team will feel afraid of them as they watch.

The All Blacks play countries from around the world, but there are lots of other rugby teams in New Zealand. Each area of the country has its own rugby team and these teams play each other in the National Provincial Championships.

The beginning of the Ka Mate haka

Te Rauparaha was an important Māori chief[13]. He often fought with other Māori chiefs. One day, Te Rauparaha was running away from some of these chiefs. He ran to the village of Motuopuhi and to the home of his friend, another chief named Te Wharerangi. He asked his friend for help. Te Wharerangi told him to go under the earth and hide in a cooking hole. Te Wharerangi's wife sat over the hole. For the Māori people, this was a very strange thing to do – no Māori man ever wanted to be under a woman in this way. This is why it was a good place to hide because no one would think he could be there.

The men who were fighting Te Rauparaha arrived. From under the ground, Te Rauparaha heard them. They were talking to his friend. Te Rauparaha felt afraid.

"*Ka Mate! Ka Mate!* (I die! I die!)" he said quietly down in the hole as he listened.

Then he heard his friend speaking again.

"He went to Rangipo," Te Wharerangi told the men.

Te Rauparaha felt hope. "*Ka Ora! Ka Ora!* (I live! I live!)" he said quietly.

But at first the men didn't believe Te Wharerangi. They asked again where Te Rauparaha was. Te Rauparaha heard them.

"*Ka Mate! Ka Mate!* (I die! I die!)" he said again in the hole.

When the men finally believed his friend and went away, Te Rauparaha was very happy.

"*Ka Ora! Ka Ora!* (I live! I live!)" he said again.

He came out of the hole to thank Te Wharerangi, saying, "This is the man who allowed me to live!"

Afterward, Te Rauparaha thought of a haka dance to tell the story of his time in the hole. This is the Ka Mate haka that the All Blacks dance. It starts: "I die, I die. I live, I live."

Cricket

Another sport that is very important to Kiwis is cricket. Cricket is a summer sport. Many people go to watch it and lots of young people play it.

The New Zealand national cricket team is called the Black Caps. Like the All Blacks, they travel around the world, playing other countries, including Australia, South Africa, England, India, Pakistan, and the West Indies.

Australia is the cricket team that all countries want to win against. The New Zealand cricket team *really* wants to be better than Australia because Australia is New Zealand's neighbor.

As with rugby, there are other cricket teams in New Zealand from different areas of the country. These teams play each other between November and April in the State Championship.

ACTIVITIES

1 Match the sentences with the words in the box.

> rugby (x5)　　cricket (x3)

1　It's the most important sport in New Zealand. _rugby_
2　The national team wants to win against Australia. ....
3　The national team wears black shorts and shirts. ....
4　This sport is played in the summer in New Zealand. ....
5　This sport came to New Zealand in the 1860s. ....
6　Teams from different areas play in the National Provincial Championships. ....
7　The national team dances and shouts before a game.

....

8　Teams from different areas play in the State Championship.

....

2 Answer the questions about the Māori story on pages 32–3.
1　Who was Te Rauparaha?

....

2　Why did he need to hide?

....

3　What was unusual for Māori people about his hiding place?

....

4　What did Te Rauparaha say to himself when he was hiding?

....

Chapter 5

Adventure sports

Bungee jumping

 There are lots of different adventure sports to do in New Zealand. Bungee jumping is a famous adventure sport. The people of the island of Vanuatu in the Pacific were the first people to bungee jump. Long ago, they jumped from tall trees with vines[14] tied to their feet.

Bungee jumping as we know it today started in the United Kingdom. In 1979, some students from the Oxford University Dangerous Sports Club jumped from a bridge in Bristol, England. They were not allowed to do this and the police arrested them afterward.

A Kiwi named A. J. Hackett saw a video of the students' jumps. He wanted to do it too, and in 1987 he jumped from the Eiffel Tower in Paris, France. The police arrested him, too! But this did not stop him. As soon as he got back to New Zealand, Hackett found a place for people to try bungee jumping. This was at the Kawarau Bridge, and it was the beginning of adventure sports in New Zealand. Hackett knew bungee jumping was more or less safe. But he also knew it had to feel dangerous to be fun.

When you do a bungee jump from a bridge, you wear a harness and you wait above a river until it is time to jump. When you jump, you fall very quickly down to the river. But the elastic rope on your harness makes you stop just above the water. Because of the elastic rope, you go up again and then down again – you bounce. Then at last you stop and you wait for someone to come and get you. It all happens very quickly.

FACT

The Nevis Highwire is the highest bungee jump in New Zealand. It's 134 meters tall. It takes only eight and a half seconds to fall from the top to just above the river.

Rona and the moon

Rona lived with her husband in a small village beside a river. Rona loved her husband, but she was a person who was often angry.

One night Rona's husband was thirsty and he asked Rona to get him a drink of water. Rona was warm and comfortable in her bed. She didn't want to get up. When her husband asked her again, she got up but there was no water in the house. Rona didn't want to walk to the river to get more water. But her husband said he was very thirsty and so she went. But she wasn't very happy about it.

Rona walked to the river in the dark. She got some water from the river, but as she was carrying it home, the moon went behind a cloud. It became very dark and Rona couldn't see. She fell over and dropped her husband's water. Rona looked up at the moon angrily.

"You cooked head!" she called it. "Why did you go away? I couldn't see without you and I fell over and dropped my husband's water!"

Rona's voice was loud and angry. The moon didn't want Rona to shout at him and he didn't like being called a "cooked head." He came angrily down from the sky and began to carry Rona away. She tried to hold on to a tree, but the moon was very strong. He pulled both Rona and the tree up into the sky with him. It was not until the next night that Rona's husband saw where she was. As he looked up at the moon, he saw her sitting there, still holding the tree. And she is still there today ...

Water sports

Since it often rains in New Zealand, a lot of water comes down from the mountains and volcanoes into the rivers. The water in the rivers is very fast, and there are many different ways to have fun on it.

One way is white-water rafting. When you do white-water rafting, you go in a boat with other people. Everyone has a paddle and as the boat travels through the fast water, everyone uses their paddle to try to stop it from going under the water. You can get very wet! The Rangitata River on the South Island is the best place to go white-water rafting in New Zealand.

If you want to do something slower, or if you do not want to go in a boat with other people, you can go kayaking. Kayaks are simple boats for one person. You use a paddle to move the boat along. Beginners can go on quiet rivers like the Whanganui River on the North Island. You can also go kayaking in the ocean. Kayaking is a good way to see the countryside and birds and animals.

Kiwis love boats and many children learn how to sail a boat when they are very young.

ACTIVITIES

. . . .

1 Underline the correct words in each sentence.

1 Modern bungee jumping first started in *New Zealand /*
   the United Kingdom.

2 A. J. Hackett's first bungee jump was from *the Eiffel Tower /*
   a bridge in the United Kingdom.

3 The highest bungee jump in New Zealand is on
   Vanatua Island / the Nevis Highwire.

4 The best place for white-water rafting in New Zealand is in
   the Whanganui River / the Rangitata River.

5 A kayak is a boat for *a group of people / one person.*

2 What do the <u>underlined</u> words refer to in these lines from
the text?

> the fall   ~~jump from a bridge~~   the water
> bungee jumping   the Rangitata River

1 They were not allowed to do <u>this</u> (page 36)
   jump from a bridge

2 <u>it</u> had to feel dangerous to be fun (page 36)
   ....

3 <u>it</u> takes only eight and a half seconds (page 37)
   ....

4 there are many different ways to have fun on <u>it</u> (page 39)
   ....

5 <u>the best place</u> to go white-water rafting in New Zealand
   (page 40) ....

Chapter 6

The arts

Painting

The Europeans who first came to live in New Zealand were not very interested in the arts. These people had to work hard to build a life in their new country. By the 1900s there were some art schools in New Zealand, but many artists left to study art in Great Britain and Europe. When these artists returned to New Zealand, they brought exciting ideas with them.

Colin McCahon (1919–87) was one of New Zealand's most famous artists. He often used words in his pictures. He also used the countryside of New Zealand in his paintings. He made Kiwis look at their country the way he did.

Another famous New Zealand artist is the Māori painter Ralph Hotere, who was born in 1931. You can see both western and Māori art in his paintings. He often uses unusual things in his work.

When New Zealand's sculptors make their work, they often think of the country's landscape, stories, and culture. The sculpture[15] of Pania is a famous tourist attraction in Napier, on the North Island. The sculptor used a Māori teenager as a model for the statue.

Pania of the reef

A long time ago, there was a beautiful woman named Pania. Pania lived in the ocean near the North Island with many other ocean people and ocean animals. Every day she swam in the ocean with her friends, and every night she went to sleep in a small river on the island.

Karitoki was the good-looking son of a Māori chief. Every evening, he went to the river to drink. One night he saw Pania, and they instantly fell in love with each other. They secretly got married, but Pania could not stay on the land all the time. So every morning she went to the ocean, and every evening she came back to her house on land.

But Karitoki wasn't happy. He wanted his wife to live on the land all the time. Karitoki and Pania argued and she ran back to the ocean.

The ocean people swam all around her and then they pulled her under the water. They kept her under the ocean with them because they didn't want her to return to the man she loved.

When you look into the water, some people say you can still see Pania with her arms out. She's trying to get back to her husband.

Books

Katherine Mansfield (1888–1923) was a New Zealand writer. Her short stories are famous all over the world. Some of these are about growing up in Wellington. Her story *At the Bay* is about different families who live in houses on a road near the ocean. In her story, Mansfield makes us see what small-town life is like. Today New Zealand holds a short-story competition every year – the Katherine Mansfield Award – named after their famous writer.

Patricia Grace, born in 1937, and Keri Hulme, born in 1947, are Māori writers. Grace writes books and short stories for adults and children. Her first book was a book of short stories called *Waiariki*, or "Hot Springs." In the stories, Grace tries to show the world who the Māori people are. Hulme's book *The Bone People* won prizes in New Zealand and Great Britain. It is also about the Māori people, their culture, and their problems.

Movies

The most famous movies made in New Zealand are the three The Lord of the Rings movies – *The Fellowship of the Ring*, *The Two Towers*, and *The Return of the King*.

J. R. R. Tolkien (1892–1973), an English writer, wrote the books in the 1930s and 40s. The stories are about a place called Middle-earth. Peter Jackson, born in 1961, a New Zealand movie director, thought the countryside of New Zealand was just right for Middle-earth. So he decided to make all the movies in New Zealand. When people saw the movies, many of them wanted to come to New Zealand to see the countryside and the mountains. The movies were very good for tourism!

FACT

**1,600 pairs of rubber ears and feet were used to make
The Lord of the Rings movies.**

A famous female movie maker from New Zealand is
Jane Campion. She was born in 1954. She made *An Angel
at my Table* which won a special prize at the Venice Film
Festival. She also made *The Piano* which won three Oscars.
Another famous female movie maker from New Zealand
is Niki Caro, born in 1967, who made *Whale Rider*. *Whale
Rider* is about a Māori girl, Pai, and her grandfather. Pai's
grandfather thinks boys are more important than girls, but
in the story Pai shows him girls can be just as smart as boys.

Music

If you listen to a lot of New Zealand's pop music, you can
hear Māori and Polynesian music together with European
and American music – all in one song. This makes

New Zealand's music special. People like lots of different pop music – rock, hip-hop, and reggae, but in all of it you can hear Māori and Polynesian music, too. New Zealand music used to follow British  fashions, but it does not anymore. New Zealand musicians are not afraid to try something new and exciting. Flight of the Conchords is a famous New Zealand group of two men who sing funny songs.

Lots of New Zealanders also like classical music and opera. Dame Kiri Te Kanawa, born in 1944, is a very famous New Zealand opera singer. She is half-Māori. Te Kanawa sings all over the world. The Kiri Te Kanawa Foundation helps good young New Zealand singers and musicians by, for example, paying for music classes.

ACTIVITIES

1 Complete the sentences with the names in the box.

> Niki Carol   Colin McCahon   Peter Jackson
> Dame Kiri Te Kanawa   Katherine Mansfield (x2)
> ~~Flight of the Conchords~~   Keri Hulme

1 *Flight of the Conchords* is a group which sings funny songs.
2 .... is a half-Māori opera singer.
3 .... directed The Lord of the Rings movies.
4 .... has a competition named after her.
5 .... is famous for her short stories.
6 .... made a movie about a Māori girl and her grandfather.
7 .... used words in his pictures.
8 .... wrote a book called *The Bone People*.

2 Match the characters in the box, from the Māori stories in Chapters 5 and 6, with the sentences.

> Rona (x3)   Pania (x3)

1 *Pania* gets married in secret.
2 .... is in love.
3 .... is often angry.
4 .... lives in water.
5 .... lives in a village next to a river.
6 .... argues with her husband.

47

Chapter 7

City life

Wellington ────────────────

New Zealand's capital city is Wellington. Wellington is New Zealand's third-largest city and is at the bottom of the North Island. The Māori have a story that the area of Wellington is the head of the fish pulled out of the ocean by Maui and that Wellington harbor is one of the fish's eyes. The Māori were the first people to go and live in Wellington, and then Europeans came to live in the city in 1839.

The city of Wellington has hills and the ocean around it. This means that a large number of people live in a small area and there is nowhere else to build houses. Some of the streets go up very high hills. If you walk to the top of these hills, you can see all around the city. Kiwis often call the city "Windy Wellington" because it is very windy.

Wellington is a small city, but it is full of life. You can walk around it, which is a good way to see all the interesting buildings and stores.

The busy harbor is beautiful and boats come and go to the South Island across the Cook Strait. There are many art galleries and lots of people go to them. The Museum of New Zealand is in Wellington and here, visitors can learn about the country's history and see works of art. There is an Arts Festival every two years and Wellington is home to the New Zealand Symphony Orchestra and the Royal New Zealand Ballet.

Every September, the people of Wellington go to The World of Wearable Art. This is a very different evening

where models wear very special clothes. People make them out of very unusual things – even phones or food!

Wellington is also home to many of New Zealand's movie studios. People who like movies call the city "Wellywood."

There is a busy café culture in Wellington – maybe people like to go into cafés to get out of the wind.

FACT

There are more cafés per person in Wellington than in New York!

Auckland

Auckland, also on the North Island, is New Zealand's biggest city. It is also New Zealand's most important city for business. Over 1.3 million people live in Auckland – that's almost a third of the people who live in New Zealand.

Auckland has warm but wet weather. There are volcanoes all around it. It is lucky that these volcanoes are not active! There are beaches on both sides of the city and there are so many boats Auckland is sometimes called "The City of Sails." Every February, up to six hundred boats take part in the Auckland Anniversary Regatta.

The Māori first came to the Auckland area in about 1350. There are still large numbers of Māori living in the city, but today Auckland is a very different city from the city these early Māori lived in. It is very busy.

As well as Māori, Europeans, and Asians, lots of people from Polynesia live in Auckland. This means that there are many different cultures in the city, each with its own stores and restaurants. Lots of young Kiwis come from the country to live in Auckland. These young people want to find work and they are excited by the idea of living in a city. There are also a large number of students. Some are studying at the colleges in the city. Others are learning English at one of the many language schools. If you want to watch important sports games, like the All Blacks playing rugby, Auckland is the place to go. If you enjoy adventure sports, you do not even need to leave the city to do them. You can do a sky jump from Auckland's Sky Tower, which is 328 meters high.

In Auckland, the country is very close to the city. It takes ten minutes to drive out to somewhere beautiful.

Christchurch

Christchurch, on the east coast of the South Island, is the second-largest city in New Zealand. It is quieter than Wellington and Auckland, but like Auckland, it has a big airport. Tourism is very important to the city.

Also like Auckland and Wellington, Christchurch is next to the ocean. The River Avon goes right through the city. Visitors and office workers sit by the river to eat their lunch and, for some money, you can take a boat down the river.

There are so many parks and gardens in Christchurch,

it is often called "The Garden City." In the spring, there are flowers everywhere.

In the summer in Christchurch, there is often music outside. In the winter there is snow on the hills, and there are good places to ski a few kilometers away. You can do most adventure sports close to the city. If you live or stay in Christchurch, you can go skiing and surfing on the same day if you want to, since both the mountains and the ocean are so close!

How a priest's dream saved a village

Once there was an old Māori priest[16]. He lived safely in a house on a hill, above a village. The village was near the ocean.

The priest knew many things about the world. At night, he often had dreams and he knew that his ancestors[17] were speaking to him through these dreams. In the old days people came to learn from the priest, but now they weren't interested in what he had to say. The children in the village didn't even know who he was. This made the old man feel very sad.

One night, just before the Māori New Year, the priest had a dream. In the dream, he saw the earth moving. A great animal came out of the earth and ran through the village. It destroyed houses and gardens and it killed many people. Then it went into the ocean. Soon after, a big wave came up out of the water. The wave destroyed everything. The only person who wasn't killed was a boy who stood in front of the ocean with his arms out.

When the priest woke up, he was very worried and he went down to the village to tell the people about his dream.

"You have to leave here quickly," he told them. "A big wave is coming. It will destroy your houses."

But nobody wanted to listen to him. Then the old man saw Turi, a village boy. He knew he was the young man from his dream.

"Make them listen," he told Turi.

Turi knew it was important to do as the priest asked and he tried to talk to the people.

"We have to listen to that old man," he told them. "I believe what he says."

The people looked away. They didn't want to hear what Turi said. But Turi's father was happy with Turi.

"You spoke well, my son," he said. "In the past people *did* listen to the old man. He was very important to us. Let's go and see him tomorrow. It's New Year. We can take some food with us."

The next day they went up the hill. Lots of people from the village decided to go with them. They found the priest and everyone ate together. For the priest it was like the old days, and he was very happy.

Then suddenly there was a great noise. The earth started to move and everyone was afraid. As they watched, safe on the hill, a great wave came from the ocean. It was so big it destroyed everything below. Soon there was nothing left. The priest's dream was now real.

Over the next year, the people began to build their village again. The priest helped the people and once again they wanted to learn from him. The old man was happy again.

ACTIVITIES

1 Complete the sentences with the cities in the box.

> Wellington (x4)   Auckland (x3)   Christchurch (x2)

1 _Wellington_ is the third-largest city in New Zealand.
2 Just under a third of New Zealanders live in ....
3 From .... , you can go skiing and surfing on the same day.
4 .... is called "The Garden City."
5 New Zealand's movie studios are in ....
6 There are beaches on both sides of ....
7 There is an Arts Festival in .... every two years.
8 .... is a very windy city.
9 .... is the biggest city in New Zealand.

2 Put the sentences about the Māori story on pages 53–5 in order.

1 A big wave destroys the village. ☐
2 People want to learn from the priest again. ☐
3 The priest has a dream about something terrible that's going to happen. ☐
4 The priest is sad because people aren't interested in him anymore. ☐ *1*
5 The priest tells the people in the village about his dream. ☐
6 Turi and his father visit the priest. ☐
7 Turi tells people to listen to the priest. ☐

Chapter 8

Traveling

Kiwis love to travel to other countries. Young people in their twenties often leave New Zealand for an Overseas Experience (or OE). They usually work at the same time. Young Kiwis often do their OE after they have finished college. They go to Australia, the United Kingdom, or Europe. Over the last few years, they have also started to go to Asian countries like South Korea or Japan. There many of them teach English.

OEs can be for a few months, a year or two, or sometimes for the rest of a Kiwi's life! Many young Kiwis decide to go to live in another country. New Zealand is very beautiful, but for some people it is just too quiet. About 4,500 Kiwis leave New Zealand every year. Many of them go to live in Australia.

FACT

One in ten New Zealanders lives in Australia.

Some people leave New Zealand but then come back. Sometimes they marry and when they return they bring their wives, husbands, and children with them.

But if some people think New Zealand is too quiet, others want to live there *because* it is a quiet country. They come to New Zealand on vacation and they love it! They then decide they want to live there. As they get off the plane to begin their new lives in a new country, maybe they feel as excited as the Māori did when they first arrived from Polynesia in their waka!

How Reitu and Reipae stayed together

Once two beautiful sisters named Reitu and Reipae lived in a village by the Waikato river. The sisters loved each other very much and did everything together.

One day, a chief named Ueoneone was traveling through the area. He saw Reitu and fell in love with her. But he went home without telling her. When he got to his village, Ueoneone couldn't stop thinking about Reitu. He knew he wanted to marry her, so he sent his magic bird to look for her. The bird flew to the sisters' village. The bird told Reitu about Ueoneone and asked if she wanted to marry him. Reitu agreed, but said her sister had to go with her. The bird asked the sisters to touch his wings. And as soon as they did this, they both became small enough to sit on the bird's back.

The bird began to fly north. After a few hours, they stopped to rest. But when Reipae got off, the bird flew back up into the sky with Reitu, leaving Reipae behind. Reitu was very angry. As soon as she saw Ueoneone, she told him to send the bird back to get Reipae.

"I can't," said Ueoneone. "Look, the bird is dying. He has no more magic."

Reitu was sad.

"Now I have lost the person I love the most in the world," she said.

Ueoneone took Reitu's hand.

"I will send my fastest men to find your sister," he told her.

The men found Reipae and brought her to Reitu. The sisters were very happy to see each other again. Reitu and Ueoneone married. Reipae also married another chief from the area, so the sisters were able to stay close for the rest of their lives.

ACTIVITIES

1 Are the sentences true (*T*) or false (*F*)?

1 Not many young people from New Zealand choose the United Kingdom for their Overseas Experience (OE). ☐ F

2 New Zealanders don't usually work during their OE. ☐

3 Kiwis also now go to South Korea and Japan for their OE. ☐

4 Every year, 45,000 Kiwis decide to go and live in another country. ☐

5 One in seven New Zealanders lives in Australia. ☐

6 Some people move to New Zealand because it's a quiet place. ☐

2 Answer the questions about the Māori story on page 59.

1 How did Ueoneone feel when he first saw Reitu?

....

2 What did the magic bird ask Reitu?

....

3 What happened when the sisters touched the bird?

....

4 How was Reipae left behind?

....

5 Why couldn't Ueoneone send the magic bird back to get Reipae?

....

6 How did the story end?

....

Glossary

[1]**magic** (page 7) *noun*   special powers that can make things happen that seem impossible

[2]**volcano** (page 8) *noun*   a mountain with a large hole at the top which sometimes explodes

[3]**anchor** (page 8) *noun*   a heavy, metal object that is dropped into water to stop a boat from moving

[4]**culture** (page 10) *noun*   the habits, traditions, and beliefs of a country or group of people

[5]**carve** (page 11) *verb*   to make an object or shape by cutting wood or stone

[6]**weave** (page 12) *verb*   to make cloth by crossing threads under and over each other

[7]**bat** (page 15) *noun*   a small animal, like a mouse with wings, which flies at night

[8]**endangered** (page 16) *adjective*   animals or plants which may soon not exist because there are now only a few alive

[9]**swamp** (page 18) *noun*   an area of very wet, soft land

[10]**hut** (page 25) *noun*   a small, simple building, often made of wood

[11]**path** (page 26) *noun*   a long, thin area of ground for people to walk along

[12]**active** (page 27) *adjective*   an **active volcano** could throw out rocks, fire, etc. at any time

[13]**chief** (page 32) *noun*   the leader of a group

[14]**vine** (page 36) *noun*   a long climbing plant

[15]**sculpture** (page 42) *noun*   a piece of art that is made from stone, wood, clay, etc.

[16]**priest** (page 53) *noun*   someone who performs religious duties and ceremonies

[17]**ancestor** (page 53) *noun*   a person in your family who lived a long time ago

The authors and publishers are grateful to the following for permission to use copyright material. All efforts have been made to contact the copyright holders of material reproduced in this book which belongs to third parties, and citations are given for the sources. We welcome approaches from any copyright holders whom we have not been able to trace but who find that their material has been reproduced herein.

p6 ©PhotoNewZealand/Arno Gasteiger; p9 ©The Natural History Museum, London; p11 ©PhotoNewZealand/Michael Hall; p12 ©focusnewzealand.com/ Graeme Mitchell-Anyon; p14 shutterstock/©Ken Brown; p19 ©The Natural History Museum, London; p20 ©PhotoNewZealand/Barbara Todd/Hedgehog House; p21 ©focusnewzealand.com/Jo Mertens; p23 istockphoto.com/©Adam Booth; p25 ©focusnewzealand.com/Black Robin Photography; p27 istockphoto.com/ ©Yvette Sandham; p28 ©PhotoNewZealand/Colin Monteath/Hedgehog House; p30 istockphoto.com/© Graeme Purdy; p31 ©FotoWare a.s 1997–2003. All rights reserved; p34 istockphoto.com/©Daniel Cooper; p36 istockphoto.com/©Ryan Johnson; p37 ©Cover/Jeremy Bright/Robert Harding; p39 istockphoto.com/ ©quidnunc; p40 istockphoto.com/©Eric Delmar; p42 ©PhotoNewZealand/ Paul Kennedy; P45 istockphoto.com/©Robert Churchill; p46 ©Getty Jamilla Rosa Cochran/Contributor (Conchords) & ©Hulton-Deutsch Collection/CORBIS (Te Kanawa); p49 shutterstock/©Chris Howey; p51 shutterstock/©bhone; p52 ©PhotoNewZealand/Gerhard Egger; p58 istockphoto.com/©Matejay (Eiffel Tower), ©Ginaellen/dreamstime.com (Korean lanterns), & istockphoto.com/ ©ROMAOSLO

Thanks to Rahera Meinders for her assistance with Māori spelling, pronunciation and culture.